John Osteen

You Can
Change Your
Destiny

BOOKS BY JOHN OSTEEN

A Miracle For Your Marriage
A Place Called There
ABC's of Faith
Believing God For Your Loved Ones
Deception! Recognizing True and False Ministries
Four Principles in Receiving From God
*Healed of Cancer *by Dodie Osteen*
*How To Claim the Benefits of the Will
How To Demonstrate Satan's Defeat
How To Flow in the Super Supernatural
How To Minister Healing to the Sick
*How To Receive Life Eternal
How To Release the Power of God
Keep What God Gives
Love & Marriage
Overcoming Hindrances To Receiving the Baptism in the Holy Spirit
Overcoming Opposition: How To Succeed in Doing the Will of God
   by Lisa Comes
*Pulling Down Strongholds
*Receive the Holy Spirit
Reigning in Life as a King
Rivers of Living Water
Saturday's Coming
Seven Facts About Prevailing Prayer
Seven Qualities of a Man of Faith
Six Lies the Devil Uses To Destroy Marriages *by Lisa Comes*
The Believer's #1 Need
The Bible Way to Spiritual Power
The Confessions of a Baptist Preacher
*The Divine Flow
*The 6th Sense...Faith
The Truth Shall Set You Free
*There Is a Miracle in Your Mouth
This Awakening Generation
Unraveling the Mystery of the Blood Covenant
*What To Do When Nothing Seems To Work
What To Do When the Tempter Comes
You Can Change Your Destiny

*Also available in Spanish

Please write for a complete list of prices in the John Osteen Faith Library
Catalog.

John Osteen Ministries • P.O. Box 23297 • Houston, Texas 77228
© 1968 John Osteen. All rights reserved.
ISBN 0-912631-17-1

Table of Contents

I. You Can Change Your Destiny 5

II. The Key To Miracles 15

III. Approaching Jesus For Deliverance 19

IV. Words That Work Wonders 31

V. Daring To Do The Impossible 41

VI. I Changed My Destiny 51

You Can Change
Your Destiny

"And Jabez was more honourable than his brethren: and his mother called his name Jabez, saying, Because I bare him with sorrow. And Jabez called on the God of Israel, saying, Oh that thou wouldest bless me indeed, and enlarge my coast, and that thine hand might be with me, and that thou wouldest keep me from evil, that it may not grieve me! And God granted him that which he requested."(I Chronicles 4:9-10)

Have you convinced yourself that your destiny is to suffer pain and disease and defeat? Have you given up and resigned yourself to the position that nothing can be done about your situation?

YOU CAN CHANGE YOUR DESTINY!

Thousands of people, who once thought there was no hope, have come into the light of God's Word and found that by daring to believe the promises of God they could revolutionize their lives.

Here in this scripture is the story of such a miracle. Jabez did what you can do. He changed his destiny. His very name tells of the condition of his life. Jabez means sorrow, pain, and trouble.

Names in the Bible have much meaning. They are meant to communicate a message in many instances. A person's name in the Bible often conveyed the type of person they were, or what they were to do for God.

The name, Jacob, meant "deceiver". He became just that. It was a picture of his life. When God changed him, He also changed his name to fit his new life. His new name was Israel, meaning "a prince".

Abram meant "high father", but God changed his name to fit his destiny. He called him Abraham, which means "father of many nations".

Moses' name told of his life, meaning "drawn out". Every time his name was called, it reminded Moses that his life had been preserved when Pharaoh's daughter drew him out of the water as a baby.

Joshua meant "savior". All the days of his life, Joshua was reminded by his name that he was a savior of his people. This is what he became as he led Israel into the promised land.

It was the same with Jabez. His mother bare him in sorrow. How? Was he crippled from birth? Was he afflicted with some weakness or disease from the beginning? Was he simply born in an atmosphere of sorrow, trouble, and heartache? Whatever the case, every time his name was called it cried out to him, "Pain! Trouble! Sorrow!"

In my imagination I picture this man convinced that this is always to be his destiny. He is confined and limited to weakness, sickness, and pain. He is convinced that this has to be his destiny for his very name spells it out.

Who can tell what went on in his mind? There must have been a constant struggle before he gave in to the fact there was no hope. No doubt someone told him of the unlimited power of the God of Israel. Faith comes by hearing the Word of God. (Romans 10:17)

I think one day he must have heard a preacher telling of God's power. I can almost hear him now as he preaches and tells how God delivered the children of Israel with signs and miracles.

I see Jabez listening to this prophet of God.

He tells of the pillar of fire by night and the cloud by day!

He tells of God's miracle manna!

He tells of God's miracle meat in the desert!

He tells of God's miracle water that came forth out of the rock!

He tells of miracle shoes and clothes that did not wear out through forty years of wandering in the desert!

He tells how God miraculously healed two million

sick, weak, and downtrodden slaves as they came out of Egypt. "There was not one feeble person among their tribes." (Psalm 105:37)

I hear this preacher cry out with Jeremiah, "Ah Lord God! behold, thou hast made the heaven and the earth by thy great power and stretched out arm, and there is NOTHING TOO HARD FOR THEE." (Jeremiah 32:17)

I hear this man declare the promise of God, "Call unto me, and I will answer thee, and shew thee GREAT AND MIGHTY THINGS, which thou knowest not." (Jeremiah 33:3)

When Jabez heard these things, hope began to rise up within him. He realized that WITH GOD ALL THINGS ARE POSSIBLE.

When he saw God's truth, he rebelled against the devil's lie!

When he saw God's light, he rebelled against the darkness!

When he saw God's life, he rebelled against disease and death!

When he saw God's liberty, he rebelled against bondage!

His faith caused him to cry out. He became angry at his so-called destiny. He rebelled! As he rose up in faith, he changed his destiny!

Listen to the record of this miracle.

"And Jabez called on the God of Israel, saying, Oh that thou wouldest bless me indeed, and ENLARGE MY COAST, and that thine hand might be with me, and that thou wouldest keep me from evil, that it may not grieve me! AND GOD GRANTED HIM THAT WHICH HE REQUESTED."

Jabez wanted God to bless him, but he wanted more. He wanted to be loosed and freed. "Enlarge my coast! Deliver me from the confining walls of fear, disease, defeat, and pain. Enlarge my coast! Get me out of this wheelchair! Raise me up from this bed! Open these doors! Break down these iron gates! ENLARGE MY COAST!"

God granted to Jabez that which he requested.

Jabez said something very important in his prayer. He prayed that God would keep him from evil. He was saying, in effect, that he wanted to be healed and delivered in order to serve God. He did not want to use his freedom from fear, sickness, and trouble to serve the devil.

JABEZ CHANGED HIS DESTINY BY CALLING UPON GOD.

You can change the whole course of your life by looking at the promises of God and daring to believe them. "And ye shall know the truth, and the truth shall make you free." (John 8:32)

The first step to healing and miracles is to see God's truth in the Bible.

A lady who was greatly afflicted in her body told me one day how she was finally healed by the miracle-working power of God.

She said, "Brother Osteen, I read the promises of God over and over and over until I suddenly saw that GOD WANTED TO HEAL ME." She said that when she saw that God really wanted to heal her, it was easy to have faith. Today she is perfectly normal.

God does not want you sick. He does not want you to suffer in pain. Your trouble and sorrow did not come from your loving Heavenly Father. "An enemy hath done this." (Matthew 13:28)

Jesus said, "The thief (Satan) cometh not, but for to steal, and to kill, and to destroy: I am come that they might have life, and that they might have it more abundantly." (John 10:10)

It is the devil who tries to steal your health, kill your body with sickness, and destroy your soul in hell.

Jesus came that you might have life and have it more abundantly. This is your hour to enjoy abundant life. The will of God is that you might prosper and be in HEALTH even as your soul prospers. (III John 2)

Jesus came all the way from heaven to bring you deliverance. When He came, He came for YOU. When He died, He died for YOU.

"Surely He has borne our griefs—sickness, weakness and distress—and carried our sorrows and pain . . . and with the stripes that wounded Him we are healed and made whole." (Isaiah 53:4-5, Amplified)

"Himself took OUR infirmities, and bare OUR sicknesses." (Matthew 8:17) "Who healeth all THY diseases." (Psalm 103:3)

Just as He bore your sins, Jesus bore your sicknesses. It is not God's will for you to bear your sins and it is not His will for you to bear your sicknesses.

Your sorrow, pain, sickness, and trouble are from the devil.

"For this purpose the Son of God was manifested, that he might destroy the works of the devil." (I John 3:8) "Resist the devil, and he will flee from you." (James 4:7)

Rise up in faith! Rebel against that sickness and disease!

Take these promises and climb up into the presence of God! Change your destiny by calling upon the God of miracles!

God is saying to you now: "Call unto me, and I will answer thee, and shew thee great and mighty things, which thou knowest not." (Jeremiah 33:3)

"If ye shall ask any thing in My Name, I will do it." (John 14:14)

"But my God shall supply all your need according to his riches in glory by Christ Jesus." (Philippians 4:19)

I have seen multitudes change their destiny by believing these promises and rebelling against the devil. Crippled, blind, deaf, and all manner of sick people have been delivered as they called upon God in faith.

YOU WILL NEVER BE HEALED AS LONG AS YOU THINK GOD WANTS YOU TO BE SICK.

You must see that it is the devil who wants you to suffer. It is God who wants you to be well.

Do not quietly accept your sickness, sorrow, trouble, or circumstances.

Get angry at the devil! Rebel in your heart against what he has brought into your life! Unless you do, you cannot be delivered.

When I was conducting a meeting in a city auditorium, I saw a crippled woman in one of the restaurants. I introduced myself to her. I told her the story of Jesus, who had not changed, but was still longing to heal the sick as in the Bible. I shared with her about the healing of my own daughter, and other miracles.

When I finished, she said, "Why Brother Osteen, I am a Christian and if God wants me this way, I am perfectly willing to suffer for Him." She felt that God had given her the crippling disease and that she was pleasing Him by suffering. Unless she changes her thinking, she will go to her grave in that condition.

That night in the service, I told the same good news about Jesus, and someone there took a different attitude.

There was a young girl who was afflicted with a club foot. She heard the truth. She realized it was the work of the devil. She rebelled against him. She cried unto the Lord. Jesus healed her instantly and she hurried to the platform to tell of her miracle! SHE CHANGED HER DESTINY FROM BEING A HOPELESS CRIPPLE!

God will not heal you and deliver you to serve the devil. Jabez continued to pray like this: "Lord, that thine hand might be with me and keep me from evil, that it might not grieve me." Jabez wanted to serve and please God. Pour your heart out to God. Press in to touch the hem of His garment. Do not be stopped or discouraged. God wants you to have ABUNDANT LIFE.

The Bible says, "God granted him that which he requested." Hallelujah! Jabez was free! He would not believe it was his destiny to go through life with pain and sorrow. He turned his eyes away from his name to the NAME OF THE GREAT JEHOVAH GOD who had declared, "I am the Lord that healeth thee." (Exodus 15:26) HE CHANGED HIS DESTINY AND SO CAN YOU!

The Lord Jesus is with you as you read these promises of His power and willingness to deliver you.

Begin to praise Him right now for your healing and victory. Praise Him while you feel pain, sorrow, disease, and heartache.

NOW ARISE AND WALK IN JESUS' NAME. Get out of bed in Jesus' Name! Begin to do what you could not do before! Act your faith! Act as though God told you the truth. Make no plans to be sick. Confess healing to those you meet. Give God the glory and serve Him in good health.

CHAPTER II

The Key To Miracles

If you want what the people in the Bible received from Jesus then you must do what the people in the Bible did.

"Jesus Christ the same yesterday, and today, and for ever." (Hebrews 13:8)

When the truth of this statement sinks into your spirit, it will eliminate your fears and doubts about healing.

This scripture tells us about Jesus. It declares something about what He was in the past, what He will always be in the future, and WHAT HE IS THIS VERY DAY! What kind of person was Jesus? Wouldn't you agree that He was a Healer of the sick? No one could read the Bible and doubt this. Matthew 9:35 says, "And Jesus went about all the cities and villages, teaching in their synagogues, and preaching the gospel of the kingdom, and healing EVERY SICKNESS AND EVERY DISEASE among the people." If He is the same today, then there is hope for you and every sick person. Mark 6:56 declares, "And whithersoever he entered, into villages, or cities, or country, they laid the sick in the streets, and besought him that they might touch if it were but the border of his garment: and as many as TOUCHED HIM were made whole." Jesus was a Healer.

What He was yesterday, He is today.

Doubt, if you will, that the stars make their stately march across the heavens and that the sun shines in all its glory, but do not doubt that God told you the truth about Jesus—He is the same yesterday, today, and forever!

If Jesus is the same today, then why are all sick people not healed? I might ask another question. If Jesus still saves, why are all sinners not saved today?

Only sinners who hear the truth and who accept and act upon that truth are saved. If they do not believe God and accept Jesus, it is not God's fault. It does not mean Jesus has changed or lost His power to save. In like manner, if a person is to be healed he must hear the truth and act upon it.

If as little truth had been preached about salvation as there has been about healing, very few sinners would be saved.

"And ye shall know the truth, and the truth shall make you free." (John 8:32) No sinner can be saved by such a message as, "It may not be God's will to save you. God used to save sinners, but He has changed. He now saves a few, but He may want you to stay lost to learn a few lessons. Be sure, therefore, to pray like this, 'Lord, if it be thy will, save me'."

Wouldn't that be a foolish way to preach! No one would believe and be saved. But this is exactly what has been done in the matter of healing. People have not been told the truth about healing. If they do not know the truth, they cannot be set free. The purpose of this book is to help you know the truth about Jesus, His power, and His willingness to heal you.

Here is a statement I want engraved upon your spirit. Read it again and again. Be sure you understand it.

IF YOU WANT WHAT PEOPLE IN THE BIBLE RECEIVED FROM JESUS, YOU MUST DO WHAT THE PEOPLE IN THE BIBLE DID.

No sinner will get what the publican did until he, like the publican, repents and says in effect, "God, be merciful to me a sinner." Sinners get salvation from Jesus because they do what sinners in the Bible did—confess, repent, and turn to God for mercy. Unless a sinner today does that, no matter how loud he may cry, he will not get what they got—that is, forgiveness and salvation.

This is true in healing also.

Jesus has not changed. He is the same. IF WE WANT WHAT SICK PEOPLE RECEIVED FROM JESUS IN THE BIBLE, WE MUST DO WHAT THEY DID. Do we marvel if a sinner is not saved because he refuses to come God's way? Then why should we marvel that a sick person is not healed who does not follow the Bible pattern? If you who are sick will do for Jesus, what the sick people in the Bible did, you will receive exactly what they received—HEALING. If you give Him your unbelief, like the people in Nazareth, you will get what they got—NOTHING! (Mark 6:6)

I have seen this demonstrated many, many times. I have witnessed large congregations explode with joy and faith as they understood the truth of God's Word. Service after service has been interrupted by the shouts of those healed in their seats as they decided to put this to the test. IT WORKS! God is no respecter of persons. He does not love others more than He loves you. Jesus said, "Ask, and it shall be given you; seek, and ye shall find; knock, and it shall be opened unto you: For every one that asketh receiveth; and he that seeketh findeth; and to him that knocketh it shall be opened." (Matthew 7:7-8)

God will hear YOU. You are as important to Him as anyone else. He has no favorites who know magic formulas.

MORE THAN LIKELY YOU WILL BE HEALED WHILE READING THIS BOOK. You will find in the following pages what the people in the Bible did to receive healing from Jesus. You are determined to believe God. You have faith, but you are about to learn how to loose your faith. You will receive what those in the Bible received from Jesus (healing) because you will do for Jesus what they did.

CHAPTER III

Approaching Jesus For Deliverance

"When he was come down from the mountain, great multitudes followed him. And, behold, there came a leper and worshipped him, saying, Lord, if thou wilt, thou canst make me clean. And Jesus put forth his hand, and touched him, saying, I will; be thou clean. And immediately his leprosy was cleansed." (Matthew 8:1-3)

I am convinced that Jesus did not love that leper any more than He loves you. He is the VERY SAME JESUS TODAY as He was the day this leper was healed.

If you want what the leper received, do what the leper did.

Many want what the leper received, but they are unwilling to do what he did. Hundreds who read this want what he received from Jesus, but will not receive because they only THINK they have done what he did. Let's study about this leper.

He came TO JESUS.

This man came to the right person. He came to Jesus. Jesus is the Healer. You cannot have healing without the healer; the benefit without the benefactor; the blessing without the blesser. You cannot separate the gift from the giver! The man or woman who prays for you cannot heal. Only God can heal. Come to Jesus. He is full of compassion and mercy. He bore your sins and sicknesses on the cross. (Matthew 8:17)

YOU CANNOT HAVE HEALING WITHOUT THE HEALER!

If you have a serious illness and choose to call your doctor, you would not have someone meet him at the front door and refuse to let him in, would you? He could do no good unless you let him in.

Do not bar the door of your heart against Jesus. Let Him in.

If you send for a doctor and let him in the front door, but refuse to let him into the bedroom where the patient is, he can do very little good. Our hearts have many rooms. Some are locked and barred with bad memories, unconfessed sin, bitterness and other things. Open wide every room to Jesus. HE CANNOT DO YOU ANY GOOD UNTIL YOU LET HIM GO WHERE THE TROUBLE IS.

In a recent crusade, a child about ten years of age came on the platform for prayer. She had been afflicted since she was a baby. All the people could see her limp across the platform as she came toward me. One leg was 1-1/2 inches shorter than the other.

She was not a Christian. She had never let Jesus come into her heart. She was willing, however, to do as the leper. As I laid my hands on her head she opened her heart and accepted Jesus as her personal Savior. I then asked God for a miracle in the Name of Jesus. She arose and walked a few steps. She turned to come back. Her own words were, "Brother Osteen, I felt my leg grow out as I walked away. I think they are both the same length." We had her sitting in a chair for prayer. We had measured her legs and the congregation had seen the difference. Now she sat down again. When the congregation saw her legs were the same length, they broke forth in a mighty volume of praise to God. She had done what the leper did and received—HEALING!

But you may have accepted Jesus and are still sick. I, too, had received Him as Savior and had preached many years, yet I had a serious condition in my stomach—ulcers. Why was I not healed? Did I not have Jesus? Yes, I had invited Him in the front door, but many rooms were barred to Him. I did not desire to discuss them.

I believed the days of miracles were over.

I shunned healing services and so-called "divine healers" as I would a rattlesnake.

I felt it was beneath my dignity, as a Southern Baptist preacher, to be caught casting out demons. Besides, I didn't know whether I really believed in demons or not.

It embarrassed me to get around those Pentecostals who were always lifting their hands and praising the Lord.

I felt those who spoke in tongues were emotional people who lacked a little in mentality!

I believed this way even though I had accepted Jesus and sought to serve Him. You see, many rooms were barred to Him. Many rooms needed cleaning.

When I was baptized in the Holy Ghost and spoke in tongues, I unlocked every door and opened them wide so Jesus would have free access to ALL MY HEART. Praise the Lord! Wherever the Healer comes, there is healing. I don't remember when I was healed, but I suddenly discovered I no longer had ulcers! That was years ago and I am still healed.

This leper did more than just come to Jesus. HE CAME HUMBLY. He came (as Mark and Luke record it) beseeching Him, worshipping Him, and falling on his face before Him. I humbled myself and fell before the Lord. I lifted my hands and heart in adoration and praise to His holy Name and healing came. "Let every thing that hath breath praise the Lord. Praise ye the Lord." (Psalm 150:6)

This leper allowed Jesus to SETTLE ALL DOUBTS about the will of God.

He had a problem, and it concerned the will of God to heal.

I can well imagine this man meeting with several other lepers. They talk about this wonderful man,

Jesus. One says, "But it is not God's will to heal people like us. We are suffering for God's glory. We are being chastened." Another says, "How could this be the will of God? This seems more like the will of HATE than the will of LOVE." Turning to the man who came to Jesus, I imagine they said, "What do you think?" He replies, "I don't know, but I think it is His will. I hope it is His will. I think I'll go ask Him and find out."

When he gets to Jesus, he says, "Lord, if you will (if it is your will), you can heal me."

Jesus didn't take long to settle that question for him and all the others. He said, "I will!" This is the only man who asked about the will of God concerning healing and Jesus settled it.

IT IS HIS WILL TO HEAL YOU!

Many want to be healed. They want what the leper received, but they do not want to take time to do what he did. He settled this question about the will of God in healing. He was convinced by the Lord that it WAS THE WILL OF GOD FOR HIM TO BE HEALED. If you, dear sick one, will do as he did, you will be healed also.

The Bible says that a double minded man is unstable in all his ways and he will not receive anything from the Lord. (James 1:7-8)

When our first daughter was born, she had signs of brain damage. The doctors said she had cerebral palsy. We could see clearly with our eyes she had something wrong with her. I had, up to this time, taken the normal attitude of denominational people about healing. I would pray, "If it be thy will . . . " I can never remember very much ever happening. Now we had to find out what the will of God was. I wasn't interested in what Jesus did for babies in the Bible, I wanted to know what He would do for MY BABY! I wanted to know the will of God.

If I wanted what the leper got, I had to do what he did. I had to settle the matter of the will of God.

I closed my library. It was filled with books telling me how miracles had passed away. I didn't want arguments AGAINST the willingness of God to heal. I wanted all the help I could get. I set my face toward God, determined to find the truth from His Word. Praise the Lord, I found it!

I discovered sickness was of the devil.

When God made Adam and Eve, He made them without blind eyes, deaf ears, afflicted limbs, and diseased organs. If He had wanted and willed these things, He would have made Adam and Eve that way.

It was the devil that caused Job's sickness. "So went Satan forth from the presence of the Lord, and smote Job with sore boils from the sole of his foot unto his crown." (Job 2:7)

Jesus said that Satan had bound the woman with a spirit of infirmity, and she was bent over and could not straighten up in a normal standing position. (Luke 13:11-16)

In Matthew 12:22, the Bible says that this man's blindness was caused by a devil.

In Mark 9:17-27 we have read the record of a boy who had convulsions and who was deaf and dumb. Jesus said it was all caused by a spirit.

Jesus healed many people. During His earthly ministry, multitudes were healed again and again as He traveled through the country. The Bible tells us all these people had been oppressed of the devil. Satan was the cause of their sickness. "How God anointed Jesus of Nazareth with the Holy Ghost and with power: who went about doing good, and healing all that were OPPRESSED OF THE DEVIL; for God was with him." (Acts 10:38)

This settled one thing in my mind. God had not afflicted our baby. This trouble came from the devil. It was not something to be coddled as a gift from God. It was something to be refused and fought as a nest of rattlesnakes!

You will never rebuke your sickness as long as you think God sent it. You will never resist it until you see it as the work of the devil. The devil wants you sick, BUT GOD WANTS YOU WELL!

The triune God is a "TRINITY OF HEALING." God is a Healer. "I am the Lord that healeth thee." (Exodus 15:26) He does not change. "I am the Lord, I change not." (Malachi 3:6)

The Lord Jesus is a Healer. The four Gospels record His mighty deeds. Hebrews 13:8 says that He is the same yesterday, today, and forever.

The Holy Ghost is a Healer. "But if the Spirit of him that raised up Jesus from the dead dwell in you, he that raised up Christ from the dead shall also quicken your MORTAL BODIES by his Spirit that dwelleth in you." (Romans 8:11)

Yes, it is the will of God to heal you. Jesus said, "For I came down from heaven, not to do mine own will, but the will of him that sent me." (John 6:38) Watch Him as He opens blind eyes and deaf ears, makes cripples leap for joy, and heals sick multitudes. What is He doing?

He is doing the WILL OF GOD!

If sickness is of God, then Jesus fought against His Father by healing the sick. Jesus said, "He that hath seen me hath seen the Father." (John 14:9) Jesus wanted to show you what God's will was about sickness—HE HEALED THEM ALL. How could it be more clear? Let God be true and every man a liar!

James 5:14-16 gives instructions about ministering to the sick. "Is ANY sick among you? let him call for the elders . . ." If it is not the will of God to heal all, how could he say ANY sick? It is God's will, so ANY sick person can expect healing.

As I sought out more on this subject I read the Psalms. I saw David pick up his harp and begin to sing Psalm 103:2-3. "Bless the Lord, O my soul, and forget not all his benefits: Who forgiveth all thine iniquities; who healeth ALL THY DISEASES."

I had always believed Jesus died for my sins, but I discovered He also died for my sicknesses. Matthew 8:17 says, "Himself took our infirmities, and BARE OUR SICKNESSES." Praise the Name of the Lord!

I, like the leper, had settled the question. We presented our afflicted baby to God KNOWING it was His will to heal her. We were no longer double minded. We did what the leper did and received what he did from the Lord—healing for our daughter! The doctor knows today that God performed a miracle in our child and healed her completely.

Stop hugging your sickness as though it was a gift from God! "Let this mind be in you, which was also in Christ Jesus." (Philippians 2:5) Christ died for your sickness! You are free! Satan has no legal right to afflict your body! The prison door is open! Walk out in Jesus' Name.

Let's face the facts.

If sickness is the will of God, then would not every physician be a law breaker, every trained nurse be defying the Almighty, every hospital a house of rebellion instead of a house of mercy? Instead of supporting hospitals, should we not do our utmost to close them? If it is not the will of God, why did Jesus command the disciples to heal the sick?

If it is not the will of God, why did Jesus say, "And these signs shall follow them that believe . . .they shall lay hands on the sick, and they shall recover." (Mark 16:17-18)

If it is not the will of God, Jesus should have said, "What things soever ye desire (EXCEPT HEALING), when ye pray, believe that ye receive them, and ye shall have them." (Mark 11:24)

If it is not the will of God to heal, we ought not to seek healing by any means—natural or supernatural.

If sickness glorifies God, we ought to pray to get sick instead of to get well.

If it is not the will of God to heal, then Jesus violated His Father's will because He healed people everywhere He went.

Praise the Lord, we know from the Word that it is the will of God to heal ALL the sick. That includes YOU. You will not get what the leper did unless you do what he did. Settle this matter in your mind. Say from your heart, "It is the will of God for me to be well!"

I preached this message in one of our northern cities. A Baptist preacher came to me later to discuss it. He said he had done all these things, but he was still not healed. He concluded, therefore, I was not preaching the truth. I asked him if he had come to Jesus. He said He had. I asked him if he had worshipped Jesus in deep humility. He said, "Yes." I said, "Are you convinced it is the will of God for you to be healed?" He hesitated, then said, "I have thought about it and have come to this conclusion. I believe God wants me to suffer some so I will have sympathy for those for whom I pray to be healed."

I said, "There is your problem. You did not get what the leper did because you haven't done what he did. The question of the will of God is not really settled in your mind."

I told him that people were not healed because of his sympathy, but because of the mercy and power of God! He listened. When he was convinced it was the will of God for him to be healed, he became overjoyed! God completely healed him that day! Hallelujah!

CHAPTER IV

Words That Work Wonders

Let us look now at another incident from the life of Jesus. The Bible tells us a centurion received something from the Lord. If we will do what he did, we will also receive.

"And when Jesus was entered into Capernaum, there came unto him a centurion, beseeching him, And saying, Lord, my servant lieth at home sick of the palsy, grievously tormented. And Jesus saith unto him, I will come and heal him. The centurion answered and said, Lord, I am not worthy that thou shouldest come under my roof: but speak the word only, and my servant shall be healed. For I am a man under authority, having soldiers under me: and I say to this man, Go, and he goeth; and to another, Come, and he cometh; and to my servant, Do this, and he doeth it. When Jesus heard it, he marvelled, and said to them that followed, Verily I say unto you, I have not found so great faith, no, not in Israel . . .And Jesus said unto the centurion, Go thy way; and as thou hast believed, so be it done unto thee. And his servant was healed in the selfsame hour." (Matthew 8:5-13)

What did this man do? He said, "Speak the WORD ONLY and my servant shall be healed!"

This centurion said, in plain language, "I do not need the actual physical presence of Jesus. All I need is His spoken Word. If I have His spoken Word I will believe it whether I see Jesus or not." Jesus said that He had not found such great faith in all Israel!

Faith is acting on the spoken Word of the Lord.

We have the spoken Word—THE BIBLE. The centurion was willing to take the WORDS of Jesus at face value. You will get what he did when you are willing to do the same.

God and His Word are one. "In the beginning was the Word, and the Word was with God, and the Word was God." (John 1:1) "For the word of God is quick, and powerful, and sharper than any twoedged sword . . . " (Hebrews 4:12) Jesus said, "The words that I speak unto you, they are spirit, and they are life." (John 6:63)

The centurion said in effect, "If Jesus says he is healed, then that settles it with me. He is healed! No more worrying! No more fretting! No more being upset! Jesus said it, and that settles it!"

Someone nearby says, "But sir, the fever—the symptoms?" I hear him laugh them off with the words, "Those things are not reliable. I have the Word of One who cannot lie. My servant shall live!"

Many people will admire the Word, read the

Word, study the Word, and defend the Word, but they will not act as though it is true.

IF YOU WANT WHAT THE PEOPLE IN THE BIBLE RECEIVED FROM JESUS, THEN DO WHAT THEY DID.

In this case, a man stepped out in faith on the spoken word of Jesus. Will you do the same? Will you act as though God told you the truth?

What has Jesus said to you? He said, "And these signs shall follow them that believe . . . they shall lay hands on the sick, and they SHALL RECOVER." (Mark 16:17-18) If the hands of a believer have been laid on you, you shall recover! Stop crying, begging, whining, and living in fear.

Isn't the Word of Jesus enough? You have asked for healing according to the Word of God.

Why are you worried? Do you think God has lied to you? Do you think His Word is no good? Face the facts! God either lied or He told you the truth!

The way you act will reveal what you believe!

Man has five senses. They are sight, hearing, taste, smell, and touch. Through these five senses he has contact with the natural world. When man wants to get in the realm of faith and touch the SUPERNATURAL world, these five senses are not to be considered. When Abraham believed God for his miracle, the Bible says, "He considered not his own body . . ." (Romans 4:19) He didn't consider what his old, wrinkled, worn-out body had to say about it. He was "fully persuaded that, what He had promised, He was able also to perform." (Romans 4:21)

The five senses cannot always be trusted. The five senses war against faith. Ignore the senses and stand on the Word of God. Your senses may tell you that you are not healed, but God's Word says, "With His stripes you are healed." (Isaiah 53:5) You have a choice to make. If you side with your senses, you are saying God's Word is not true. Which one will you believe? When you confess the Word and stand by it, you please God and receive healing.

When we prayed for our daughter, who was born abnormal, we could see no change in her, but we CONFESSED to everyone God had healed her. On what basis? Certainly not the five senses. Our eyes told us the opposite. The only basis we had was the Word of God. God kept His Word! HE ALWAYS DOES. "I will hasten my word to perform it." (Jeremiah 1:12)

A blind boy came to the altar of a church for prayer. We rebuked the blind spirit in Jesus' Name and pronounced him healed. He did not see instantly. I did not tell him to say, "I can see. I can see." That would have been falsehood. I asked him to confess the Word of God. To confess means *to say the same thing.* I asked him to say the same thing God said in His Word. God said, "They shall lay hands on the sick, and they shall recover." "With his stripes ye are healed." "I am the Lord that healeth thee." "In my name ye shall cast out demons." He began to confess—even though his senses contradicted it—"With his stripes I am healed." The next day he could see! He is normal today! Glory to God!

The Word declares that you are healed. Do as the centurion did and you will get what he got from the Lord!

Jesus said, "What things soever ye desire, WHEN YE PRAY, believe that ye receive them, and ye shall have them." (Mark 11:24) He said to believe it right when you pray—while you can still see the swelling, feel the pain, and are conscious of all the symptoms. BELIEVE WHAT GOD SAID RIGHT IN THE FACE OF ALL CONTRARY SENSE KNOWLEDGE—AND YOU SHALL HAVE THEM!

There are still signs of life in a tree immediately after it has been cut down. We do not worry because we know it has been cut down and all these signs of life will pass away in due time. When your disease has been cut down by the Lord, it is dead. Some of the symptoms may linger to convince you it is still alive and God has failed, but you know better. You confess the Word. You say what God says! The symptoms cry out, "You are NOT healed." The Word of God, who cannot lie, says, "By His stripes ye are healed." You stand with God. You confess His Word. You say the same thing that God says. You believe WHEN YOU PRAY that you have received. God said that if you will believe His Word against all these other things, you shall have your request! When you have no basis for your healing but the Word of God, that is REAL FAITH!

A well-known evangelist gave an excellent explanation of Satan's part in disease. He describes it as follows:

"Every disease has a life—a germ. That germ is from Satan because it destroys. It is what Jesus called a 'spirit of infirmity.' That germ causes the disease to grow just like the germ of life from our conception causes us to grow and become a human body. When the germ of life leaves our body, then our body will die. It will decay and return to the dust. Likewise, when the spirit of a disease leaves, the disease dies, and will decay and disappear.

"We have power over the spirit of the devil that brings disease because Jesus said: 'In my name shall they cast out devils.' In His Name we have absolute authority to command the life of disease to leave, and it must obey us. When it leaves, then the disease dies and the effects disappear.

"For example, a cancer has a life in it. That life is of the devil because it destroys and kills. As long as that life is there, that cancer-life will continue its work of destruction, but when that cancer-life is commanded to leave, in Jesus' Name, it must go; then the cancer is dead. It will decay and pass away and the sick person will recover.

"You cannot see the spirit that gives life to your disease. How do you know what happens to it? Can you believe the Word of God? He says the spirit leaves! The disease will stop growing. DECAY WILL SET IN, and it will disappear.

"Many people are healed and completely delivered from the life of their disease, BUT WHEN IT BEGINS TO DECAY, they lose faith. They feel pains, aches, and all kinds of troubles in their bodies. They don't realize it is the process of decay in the dead disease. They begin to fear and exercise unbelief. The spirit can re-enter and begin the deadly work again in that body."

DON'T CONFESS WHAT YOUR SENSES TELL YOU, BUT WHAT THE BIBLE TELLS YOU.

Remember, to confess means *to say the same thing*. When you say the same thing as God, you are confessing correctly. The SYMPTOMS say you are not healed. Don't say what they say. God says, "By His stripes ye ARE healed." Say what God says!

You may say, "If I could only see a little change." Faith is the evidence of things NOT SEEN. You don't see your healing with your natural eye, but you have evidence that you are healed. That evidence is from One who cannot lie. You have the Word of God.

Let's study another illustration. In Mark 11:12-14, Jesus rebuked a fig tree, but nothing happened immediately. I can imagine Peter and John lingering behind to see what happens to the tree. As they wait they grow more and more disappointed. NOTHING SEEMS TO HAVE HAPPENED. Nothing about the tree has changed. I can hear Peter say, "John, Jesus has performed many miracles, but I believe He failed this time. I can't see any change. I am sure He failed."

The next day, however, they are amazed to see the tree dried up from the roots. (Mark 11:20)

There are two parts to that tree—the SEEN and the UNSEEN. Peter could see the outer part of the tree, but he could not see the root system. The part he could not see was the source of the life of the tree.

It was from the roots that the tree drew its life. The roots could not be seen because they were under the ground. Now here is something to always remember. The withering, powerful, prevailing, authoritative Word of Jesus had its first effect in the realm Peter could not see—the life of the tree—the roots.

If Peter could have seen as Jesus saw, he would have known at the instant He spoke, the ROOTS WITHERED AND DIED!

There is a realm of your disease you can see and there is a realm YOU CANNOT SEE. The realm you can see is the area of sense knowledge and symptoms. The area you cannot see is the realm where the disease draws its life. The Word of God takes effect in this area first to cut off the life of the disease. Do not doubt God while the symptoms are slow in passing away. The life is cut off. In the realm you cannot see, the Word of God has had its effect! "YOU SHALL RECOVER! BY HIS STRIPES YOU ARE HEALED! RISE, TAKE UP YOUR BED AND WALK! BE MADE WHOLE."

The centurion said, "Speak the word only, and my servant shall be healed." He was willing to take the spoken Word of Jesus ALONE and act as though it was true.

IF YOU WANT TO RECEIVE WHAT PEOPLE IN THE BIBLE DID, YOU MUST DO WHAT PEOPLE IN THE BIBLE DID.

Take Jesus at His Word!

Believe He told you the truth!

Act as though He told you the truth!

When you find a person who will do what this centurion did, you will see that person get what this centurion received.

When our son, Paul, was a little boy, he had warts all over his body. My wife tried in every way she knew to treat them so they would go away. It dawned on her one day that she could pray for him to be healed.

She laid hands on him and commanded the life of those warts to leave in the Name of Jesus. She knew the Word of God had taken effect in the unseen realm. In the realm we could see, the warts still could be seen as clearly as in the past. We looked at them day by day and said in the face of their continued presence, "Devil, you are a liar. He is healed in the Name of Jesus." We rejoiced and praised God that Paul was healed. About two weeks later, our son came in all excited. Several of the warts had disappeared. Soon all of them were gone!

We received what the centurion did because we did what he did—believed and confessed the Word of God.

The Bible says, "My son, attend to my WORDS; incline thine ear unto my SAYINGS. Let them not depart from thine eyes; keep them in the midst of thine heart. For they are LIFE unto those that find them, and HEALTH to all their flesh." (Proverbs 4:20-22)

CHAPTER V

Daring To Do The Impossible

"And he entered into a ship, and passed over, and came into his own city. And, behold, they brought to him a man sick of the palsy, lying on a bed: and Jesus seeing their faith said unto the sick of the palsy; Son, be of good cheer; thy sins be forgiven thee. And, behold, certain of the scribes said within themselves, This man blasphemeth. And Jesus knowing their thoughts said, Wherefore think ye evil in your hearts? For whether is easier, to say, Thy sins be forgiven thee; or to say, Arise, and walk? But that ye may know that the Son of man hath power on earth to forgive sins, (then saith he to the sick of the palsy,) Arise, take up thy bed, and go unto thine house. And he arose, and departed to his house. But when the multitudes saw it, they marvelled, and glorified God, which had given such power unto men." (Matthew 9:1-8)

What did this man do? He ACTED on the Word of God. Jesus told him to DO what he could not do before and he did it!

I have commanded people in my meetings to DO WHAT THEY COULD NOT DO BEFORE. I have commanded blind people to see and they have seen. I have commanded deaf people to hear and they have heard. I have commanded cripples to walk and they have walked. THEY RECEIVED WHAT THIS PARALYTIC RECEIVED BECAUSE THEY DID WHAT HE DID.

When Jesus commanded Peter to let down his nets for a catch of fish, Peter hesitated. He told Jesus he had fished in those waters all night and had caught nothing. Peter was an authority on fishing. He knew those waters. It seemed useless to try again, but he said a marvelous thing. "NEVERTHELESS AT THY WORD I WILL LET DOWN THE NET." (Luke 5:5) When he acted on the Word of Jesus, he got results.

I realize that people have told you that you cannot get well. Authorities have given their verdicts. Will you, in the face of all this say, "Nevertheless, at thy Word I will act"?

Faith is an act. Believing on the Word is acting on the Word.

Faith without works is dead. (James 2:20) To say you believe, and not act as though you believe, shows you have dead faith.

One translation says, "Faith without corresponding action, is dead." It is not enough to talk your faith. You must act your faith.

The Bible says, "When Jesus saw their faith . . ."

(Mark 2:5) Faith is something you can see. If you substitute the phrase *act on the Word* for *believe* you will understand it more clearly.

"And these signs shall follow them that *act on my Word.*" (Mark 16:17) "He that *acts on my Word,* the works that I do shall he do also; and greater works than these shall he do; because I go unto my Father." (John 14:12) "All things are possible to him that *acts on my Word.*" (Mark 9:23)

Let's put it this way—HE WHO ACTS ON THE WORD HATH! That is present tense. When you act on the Word, you HAVE whatsoever you desire of God. Hope is always in the future. Acting on the Word brings it to pass NOW.

The great men and women of the Old Testament never gave much thought to the matter of having faith. However, Hebrews 11 refers to them as mighty examples of faith. These folks did not worry and fret about how to have faith. They simply heard God speak and ACTED AS THOUGH HE TOLD THEM THE TRUTH! We look back and call them men and women of faith.

Faith is acting as though God told you the truth.

How do I know Noah believed? He started acting as though God told him the truth. He started building the ark! How do I know Joshua and the Israelites believed? They started marching around the walls of Jericho! How do I know Jehoshaphat and his army believed? They began to sing and shout with joy. They acted as though God told them the truth.

How do I know this paralytic believed? When he heard Jesus say, "Arise," he acted as though he could and found out he was healed!

You can say ten thousand times a day, "I have faith," but still remain sick. Faith is an act. Start acting as though God told you the truth. Unless you do this, all else is in vain.

While preaching in the city auditorium of Tulsa, Oklahoma, I saw this wonderful truth demonstrated. I was preaching about healing, and faith was building up in the hearts of the people. As they listened to the Word of God, they began to understand. Suddenly, I challenged them to do what they couldn't do before—right then—in the Name of Jesus! In the audience sat a young girl who had a club foot. She accepted the challenge and attempted to stand normally on her crippled foot. Glory be to God for His mercy! SHE DISCOVERED IT WAS ABSOLUTELY NORMAL!

In a church in Houston, Texas, I prayed for an elderly lady who was badly afflicted with arthritis. She was stooped. She hobbled along. She could not lift her hands much higher than her waist. She used a cane to walk. As she stood before me, I commanded the demon that had bound her with this sickness to leave in the Name of Jesus! She hobbled away. She seemed no better.

Three days later, as I continued the meeting, she started to the front again to be prayed for. (I am not against people coming back again for prayer, and I do not remember ever doing this before.) I suddenly told her not to come. I told her she was healed. The demon had been cast out. She had been delivered because God promised to keep His Word. When I said these things, she turned and hobbled back to her seat.

After a few minutes a commotion began in the audience. I looked and saw a cane waving in the air. The elderly lady had decided to act as though she was healed. She started running up and down the aisle and around the church. Her arms were high in the air. WHEN SHE ACTED, GOD KEPT HIS WORD AND SHE WAS HEALED!

In one of our city-wide campaigns, I made a visit to one of the homes with a pastor. We went to pray for a lady who had a back injury. Because of this, she had lost her equilibrium. She could not stand or walk without falling over. Her sense of balance was gone. She was flat on her back in bed. If she opened her eyes, the room would go around in circles. This had persisted for about ten weeks.

We anointed her with oil and commanded the spirit of infirmity to leave. We said, "Be healed in the Name of Jesus." We laid hands on her and fully expected her to recover. When we had finished, I asked her if she thought God meant what He said. She said, "Yes." Then I told her that people who had been healed had no business in bed. I said, "Rise up and walk in the Name of Jesus!" She looked at me quizzically, but realized I meant it. Up she came with a determination to act as though God told her the truth. She stumbled a little bit, then started walking normally. When this woman ACTED she was healed.

He that acts on the Word HATH!

I have seen this demonstrated hundreds of times all over the world. When people DARE TO DO WHAT SEEMS IMPOSSIBLE they find God on the scene.

In crowds numbering into the multiplied thousands we have watched the marvelous power of God work as people ACTED THEIR FAITH. They would listen to the Gospel. They would receive Jesus into their hearts. They would begin to understand His desire for them to be well. Then they ACTED LIKE HE TOLD THEM THE TRUTH!

I have seen cripples arise and walk as the multitudes shouted and praised God. I have seen all manner of sickness and disease vanish as people acted on God's Word.

The devil tells you that you cannot walk, see, hear, or live a normal life. All the circumstances seem to agree with this. BUT YOU HAVE HEARD FROM GOD. YOU KNOW HIS PROMISES.

What are you going to do now?

DARE TO DO THE IMPOSSIBLE! DARE TO DO WHAT THE DEVIL AND CIRCUMSTANCES SAY YOU CANNOT DO!

I read the story of a dog that had the habit of chasing cars. His master decided to chain him to a tree. The dog had a hard time getting used to this limitation. He raced out after cars only to come abruptly to the end of the chain. It jerked his head terribly time and time again. He finally gave up. He decided he could just go so far and no further.

He would walk out to the end of the chain and stop. He knew by bitter experience that this was as far as he could go. He was trapped. He was limited. He was unhappy, but it was IMPOSSIBLE for him to go one step farther.

One day his master felt he had learned his lesson so he patted the dog on the head and at the same time unbuckled the collar around his neck. The dog still stayed there even though he was loosed from the collar. His master knew that he could bound out of it now with one leap.

But do you know what that dog did? He continued to walk out to his former limits and sit and long for freedom. He could still feel the collar and did not realize his master had loosened it. Little did he know that all he had to do was to TAKE ONE STEP BEYOND WHAT HE FELT WAS HIS LIMITATIONS to discover his deliverance!

But there he sits, sad and dejected!

Freed, but not free. Delivered, but not enjoying it. All he needs to do is act!

Many of you are like that. For years you have had sicknesses, fears, and limitations. Bitter experiences, apart from God's power, have convinced you that you can do just so much and no more.

But now you have read the Gospel. You know the good news.

Your MASTER came all the way from heaven to let the oppressed go free. He came to SET THE CAPTIVES FREE. "And ye shall know the truth, and the truth shall make you free." (John 8:32)

When Jesus came He broke the power of Satan. THE COLLAR IS LOOSED. He came to destroy the works of the devil. (I John 3:8) And He did!

His living words now are, "Rise, take up thy bed and walk." "Be thou made whole!" "Woman thou art LOOSED from thine infirmity!"

But thousands sit looking sad, wishing for deliverance. All you have to do is TEST THE COLLAR. You are loosed! Dare to act like it. Take that one step which seems impossible and discover that with God all things are possible!

A young Indian boy of fifteen had been afflicted from birth with club feet. He had walked on the sides of his ankles for so many years that large callouses formed. It was painful even to watch him drag himself along.

This young man stood among the thousands who gathered in our open air meeting in India. He heard what you are hearing. He received Jesus as his Savior. We told him these same things.

The "collar" had been on him since birth. He knew by bitter experience his limitations. BUT

FAITH CAME INTO HIS HEART AS HE HEARD THE WORD OF GOD. He heard about the Master coming to loose the captives.

It was a thrilling day when he decided to test the collar. In the Name of Jesus he DARED TO DO THE IMPOSSIBLE.

He discovered he was free! His feet went flat on the ground for the first time in his life. He walked! He testified! He was free!

You are free, too! You will discover it to be so by ACTING AS THOUGH GOD TOLD YOU THE TRUTH.

He said, "I am the Lord that healeth thee." "With His stripes ye are healed." "Be thou made whole in Jesus' Name."

Begin now to act your faith. Keep on acting it. God wants you well. You will not waver. You will not fail. He who acts on the Word of God HATH—hath his miracle.

CHAPTER VI

I Changed My Destiny

> (I asked my sister, Mary Givens, to share with you the following testimony of how she changed her destiny. This is one of the greatest miracles of God I have ever witnessed. I know it will bless you.)

What amazing grace is revealed by God's Spirit as we turn to the writers of the Gospels; what a thrill to our hearts as we see and watch this glorious Personality as he moves in and out blessing, helping, healing, making the day grow brighter for each, and making burdens seem less heavy as new surges of desire for better things come suddenly to our wills.

And yet, it is not to the four Gospels so much which I would call attention at this time, but to a fifth one—the one that records the healing and deliverance of someone not in the long ago, but now! He came to ME in the year 1961 in the back bedroom of a simple home at 2448 Bentley Avenue in Dallas, Texas.

I wish it was not necessary to speak of myself, but only of Him—this wonderful, personal, all-sufficient Jesus. However, the words concerning myself will be for one purpose alone—that this great and loving Jesus might be glorified for "He brought me up also out of an horrible pit, and out of the miry clay, and set my feet upon a rock, and established my goings. And he hath put a new song in my mouth, even praise unto our God: many shall see it, and fear, and shall trust in the Lord." (Psalm 40:2-3) His promise has been fulfilled. Amen!

"Thou hast put off my sackcloth, and girded me with gladness; To the end that my glory may sing praise to thee, and not be silent. O Lord my God, I will give thanks unto thee for ever." (Psalm 30:11-12)

About five years ago, after having a very severe convulsion, a brain-wave (encephalogram) and other necessary tests indicated that I was afflicted with epilepsy. A neuro-surgeon in Dallas, Texas made these tests. Treatment was begun immediately with Dilantin. This was a small tablet or pill to be taken two times each day, and I was cautioned very carefully against missing it, even for one dose.

The year prior to treatment was spent on a hospital bed in my home equipped with traction, and my neck was in a brace due to a slipped disc. After nine weeks of the Dilantin treatment I was able to concentrate, to study, and to teach—and felt I could see it through with God's help.

How drastically different this was to be I had no way of foretelling!

All previous tests of my faith seem small by

comparison with the strangeness to be known in the years ahead. Horrible nightmares, black-outs, loss of memory, and stumbling necessitated further treatment by other specialists. For a time it would seem that I was improved and I would attempt to go forward as before, but no one knew so much as I did the horrible changing of my personality. I became supersensitive to close friends and family. This resulted, usually, in arguments followed by profuse apology on my part and then forgetting all but that I had hurt someone—I did not know who, or why, or what to do about it.

Our home had always been filled with the love and laughter of friends, dear and wonderful people, but I withdrew from them. The phone rang and rang, and I would not answer. Either my head was hurting so severely that I couldn't answer, or else I was afraid to hear the words, "You do not sound like yourself!" I would want to scream, "I'm not! Help me, someone!" No one would have believed it had I said that I could no longer remember a single scripture.

"Satan hath desireth thee!"—and it seemed God was letting him have me. As my personality became different so did my concept of God, if I bothered with a concept at all. I could not reason my way to Him. Prayers were only a result of prolonged habit.

During periods of normalcy I had reasoned that God is good, His ways are not our ways, and "Think it not strange concerning the fiery trial which is to try you... But rejoice." (I Peter 4:12-13) Other servants of God—great people—had endured and suffered, so why should I be so certain I would be delivered? If God sees fit to allow this then I will change it into a glory, a testimony for Him.

And what a testimony I gave with my withdrawal!

I soon saw there was no glory for God. Satan must have called a special celebration when he attacked me this last time. I remember the coma-like state, the torment, the cries, the inability to come back to reason, the barricaded bed, fighting the nurse and my mother, and the nights sitting in bed crying, "Don't tell me there is no hell, this is it!"

All these things were related to me later. The nurse said that for two weeks I did not open my eyes, not even in all the frenzy. The doctor said an infection had begun in my head and had brought on this seizure. For weeks I was unable to walk. There was no coordination of the members of my body. One event occurred during this time which I can remember very plainly. I was so afraid I would live that I could not bear the thought. My arms were around Mother and I was pleading and crying not to have to live like this: "Pray for me. You know I cannot—I am not going to live like this. Mother (she was crying), I'll be with Hazel (my sister who had died) and I'll be all right then. We will be together. Mother knows I cannot bear it any more, don't you, Mother?"

Suddenly SOMEONE FROM WITHIN ME said, "Call John, go call John!" That is all. I know that voice was NOT MINE, but the voice of the Spirit of God—the One who never lays down the battle until victory is won!

The strange thing is that I had not seen my brother in nearly two years. We had been very close. He had won me to the Lord when only a teenager. John had taught me about God, but with his busy ministry in other places and my responsibilities, we had grown apart.

As my brother John drove along the freeway in Houston, Texas, the Lord showed him a vision of me and my condition. He told those in the car with him: "Mary is terribly sick. The Lord just told me she shall be delivered!" When he arrived home, Mother called him and he started for Dallas immediately. Before he got in the car he said he opened his Bible for a promise. As he opened the Bible, his finger pointed to the scripture, "Fear not, Mary, for thou hast found favor with God." God is so good to even call our names!

There was a sense of waiting for something, but I did not know what—something that was not bad this time. When would it come? When would it happen—whatever it was? This too, I remembered.

And they came—God's messengers—in behalf of one of His own! Brother H. C. Noah and my brother were there in the room. My reflections were, "Is this John, or Gene (my son)? Who is the other? Do I know him? Why are they here?"

There was time for no more reflection because someone was speaking and saying, "Do not tell me this is of God! God is love! God would not do this to my sister!" A bit of reasoning—enough to lift me—"Not of God? Not His will? What can it mean?"

Then I heard someone saying to me, "Get out of bed!" The words were hardly spoken until I was on my feet falling in every direction it seemed. Someone was grabbing me and holding me. They were praying and defying that one that was in the room to destroy me, telling him they knew the truth—God could and would set me free. They declared it done, pointing to the Cross and claiming its power for healing and for defeat of him that had dared to intrude on God's territory. As they prayed and hands were on my head, I heard my brother's voice. It was a language I could not translate, but neither did it seem foreign to me. It was like hearing a once familiar language, long ago forgotten. But I knew it meant the victory was won! And that voice again bade me, "Walk! You are going to walk now!"

And I did not just walk—I ran!

The nurse was frightened. Mother was jubilant! I walked, I talked, I ate, I told my husband about it, but in a sense I was shut up with God. That is the only explanation I can find for it. I was so preoccupied, so taken up with what had happened, that I only wanted to look into this thing with Him and listen and let Him tell me what it was all about.

Those about me said I had been very swollen and the glazed look in my eyes had changed my looks completely. The glazed look was gone now, however, and light was dawning—reason, true reason—love for God and for all those about me!

For two nights I remained awake—my eyes open. During this time God led me supernaturally out of

the maze of darkness and confusion back to real
sanity. I did not pray for anything. I was just awake
as if it were day—wandering in new realms, amazed,
unable to grasp such love. No wonder Paul's
vocabulary ran out when he attempted to describe it!

Each night previously, I had been tormented by
the devil. In these two nights when my eyes were
open, a very unusual event happened. It was almost
as if it were taken from the Book of Revelation—that
struggle depicted there between the good and the
evil. For there was a battle going on. I SAW
NOTHING, but I know the exact vantage point of
each. The Lord stood at my head—and the devil in
the corner of the room. The One at the head never
moved. It was just the sense of a Presence, One with
whom I felt perfectly at ease. Slowly, as if coming
through a tiny opening somewhere, there was a
light—a soft light. I asked my husband if he could
tell where the light was coming in. He even checked
the windows and the blinds. Each slat was in its
proper place. How strange, I thought, but how
wonderful. There was no illumination of articles or
furnishings. I could not tell its direction. I only knew
it was there. It was not frightening, but an easy
blending of the natural and the supernatural!

But the most unusual of all was the music—and
I know now it was from God's portals. How ever
could earth's language describe it? I know that
Heaven is not going to be a strange place at all, for
none of these things seemed strange. Though victory
was declared, there were a few battles to be fought.
I heard the music when I was most conscious of
Satan's presence there. I did not know what it was

at first. Somewhere, as though in the distance, I kept
hearing it. I asked my husband to get up and see
where the music was coming from. The neighbors
were in their yard and we decided it must be from
there. As the supernatural light grew clearer, I could
hear the music more plainly. It was a song of
rejoicing. Such victory! Such celebration! What song
was it? The nearest I can come to remembering was
The Awakening Chorus.

> Awake, awake! And sing the blessed story!
> Awake, awake! And sing the triumphant song;
> The Lord Jehovah reigns and sin is backward turned.
> Rejoice! Rejoice! Lift heart and voice: Jehovah reigns!

What inspiration! What a wonderful call of love!
The shout of the Conqueror! It seemed as if heaven
had come down to celebrate...Victory! O, the
wonder of such love! I adored Him! I raised my hands
in eagerness to praise Him with my entire being,
making Him all important—the light, the music, and
the victory!

I do not know why these special signs were given
to me. Even though I do not see the light now, it has
lighted everything for me in a magnificent way.
Neither do I hear the music, but victory is mine. He
gave me the signs when nothing else, possibly, would
have been of any use. He, my Father, was coming in
for His own!

In this experience, there was no striving to
remember anything. Muscles and nerves, so long
unaccustomed of their own volition to relax, now
were heeding their Maker. As He commanded the
waves to be still, so every part of my being stood at

attention. The Lord God of Hosts had marched in.
He had lifted His standard! There was a flash as
Someone went by. I did not see the face—but
someone left. The Lord had seen me through to
complete victory. The enemy was defeated. It was
the close of the second night and all was well. There
was no loneliness for the music nor was there the
feeling of a Presence—because I was able now, once
again, to know He was in my heart and never, never
would I be alone nor would I feel alone again. Never
would the night be so black that Heaven's
reinforcements could not get through. And I know
that if He cannot use the usual channels, He will just
make some more channels!

I felt reasoning return! I felt vitality flow through
my body. I felt alive. He healed, not just someone
long ago, but ME! It is a glorious thing to receive
deliverance. With the light of His Presence I went
from panic to peace, from restlessness to restfulness,
from void to victory, from suffering to sufficiency,
and satisfaction!

And it cost Him so much! But He is willing to
give so much—His all. Long ago He told us the ONE
sheep, the ONE piece of silver, the ONE son drew
His attention because His is a Father's heart and He
knows when one of His own is out of their place of
usefulness—and He never lets up and never rests
until we are home. What a wonderful, personal Lord
we have! I have to break all molds of concept of Him
and get greater ones.

O, thank God, I am not holding Him—HE
HOLDS ME—and those hands are scarred! Never let

me forget! For none of the ransomed ever knew how deep were the waters crossed or how dark was the night the Lord passed through ere He found the sheep that was lost!

No longer do I take Dilantin for epilepsy because I do not have epilepsy! With His stripes I am healed! Many years have passed since the Lord healed me and I am still rejoicing in His wonderful mercy and serving Him with my good health.

By MARY GIVENS

MIRACLES

Young Boy With Clubbed Feet Completely Healed

One of the greatest healing miracles I have ever witnessed was the healing of this young club-footed boy. He stood in a vast throng of thousands of people listening to the Gospel. Finally, he understood and opened his heart to Jesus. Faith arose in his heart as he learned about God's healing power, and he was completely healed.

Notice the pictures of his healed right and left feet. You can see the close-up of the callouses where he had walked on the sides of his feet all his life. Never had he been able to place his feet flat on the ground.

Notice, also, the picture of him walking to the platform to show us that God had healed ONE of his feet. You can see how he is crippled in his right foot. It was pitiful to see him hobbling along, but he was so glad to testify of the healing of his left foot. Later in the crusade, God healed the other foot! See him standing with both of them healed. Hallelujah!

I say with Jeremiah, "Ah Lord God! behold thou hast made the heaven and the earth by thy great power and stretched out arm, and there is NOTHING TOO HARD FOR THEE."

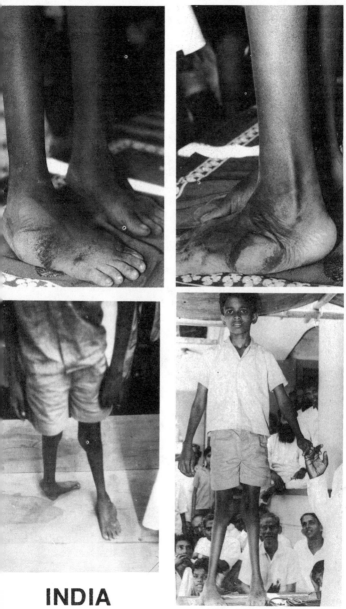

INDIA

One of the most thrilling moments in the India Crusade was the healing of this cripple. Many like him were brought to the meeting in rickshaws and lifted out to lay upon the ground. This young man lay there and listened to the Gospel. He opened his heart to Jesus and found peace and salvation. During the prayer for the sick he ACTED HIS FAITH. He began to try to get up and did so with the help of those around him. Then he began to walk alone! He came to the platform to testify of what Jesus had done for him!

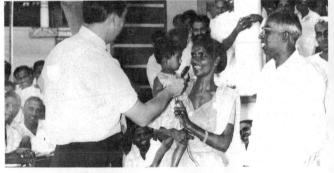

This little girl held by her mother had never heard, spoken, or walked a step in her life. When Jesus healed her she began to walk and talk for the first time. The broad smile on her mother's face tells the joy of this miracle.